STORIES OF
RELIGION

The Good
Samaritan

First published in 2008 by
Franklin Watts
338 Euston Road
London
NW1 3BH

Franklin Watts Australia
Level 17/207 Kent Street
Sydney
NSW 2000

A CIP catalogue record for this book is available
from the British Library.

ISBN 978 0 7496 8369 6 (hbk)
ISBN 978 0 7496 8375 7 (pbk)

Series Editor: Melanie Palmer
Series Advisor: Dr Barrie Wade
Series Designer: Peter Scoulding

Printed in China

Franklin Watts is a division of
Hachette Children's Books,
an Hachette Livre UK company
www.hachettelivre.co.uk

The Good Samaritan

by Anita Ganeri and Peter Utton

W

FRANKLIN WATTS

LONDON•SYDNEY

About this book

The story of the Good Samaritan comes from the Bible. The Bible is the name that Christians give to their holy book. They believe that the Bible is the word of God and that it teaches people how God wants them to live and behave. The Bible is divided into two parts, called the Old Testament and the New Testament. The 'Good Samaritan' is found in the Gospel of Luke (chapter 10; verses 25-37) in the New Testament. Jesus used the story to show how treating other people kindly, even if you do not know them, is very important in God's eyes.

One day a man asked Jesus,
"What should I do to
make God love me?"

"You must love God with all your heart," Jesus replied, "and be kind to everyone you meet."

Then Jesus told the man a story
to show him what he meant.

Once there was a man who was walking from Jerusalem to a town called Jericho.

The road was full of thieves, waiting to attack anyone who passed by.

The man had walked this way
before and never had any trouble.
This time, he was not so lucky.

As he turned the corner,
some thieves jumped out
and attacked him.

They stole his clothes and money and ran away. The man was left by the side of the road with nothing but cuts and bruises.

Later, a priest came down the road on his way to Jerusalem. Priests were supposed to help people.

But when the priest saw the injured man, he did not stop. He just looked away and crossed to the other side of the road.

Soon a second man passed by. He was also a kind of priest called a Levite. When he saw the injured man, he did not even slow down.

"It's got nothing to do with me," he said and hurried away.

Next came a man called a Samaritan riding along on a donkey.

Samaritans were hated by
most other people.

But as soon as the Samaritan saw the injured man, he stopped and got off his donkey.

Gently he cleaned the man's
wounds and carefully bandaged
them with cloth.

Then the Samaritan lifted the man onto the donkey and set off down the road.

Further on, they came to an inn where the injured man could be looked after.

Next day, the good Samaritan had to leave for Jersualem. Before he went he took out some money.

"Please take good care of my friend," he told the innkeeper. "Don't let him leave until he is better."

"If you spend more money than
this, I will pay you back the next time
I pass this way," said the Samaritan.

Then he got on his donkey
and rode away.

The innkeeper looked after the
man until he was well enough
to go home.

When the Samaritan next passed the inn he paid the innkeeper more money, just as he had promised.

Jesus finished the story and looked at the man who had asked him the question.

"The Samaritan stopped to help
the injured man, even though
he was a stranger," said Jesus.
"Now you must do the same."

Hopscotch has been specially designed to fit the requirements of the Literacy Framework. It offers real books by top authors and illustrators for children developing their reading skills.

ADVENTURES

Aladdin and the Lamp
ISBN 978 0 7496 6692 7

Blackbeard the Pirate
ISBN 978 0 7496 6690 3

George and the Dragon
ISBN 978 0 7496 6691 0

Jack the Giant-Killer
ISBN 978 0 7496 6693 4

TALES OF KING ARTHUR

1. The Sword in the Stone
ISBN 978 0 7496 6694 1

2. Arthur the King
ISBN 978 0 7496 6695 8

3. The Round Table
ISBN 978 0 7496 6697 2

4. Sir Lancelot and the Ice Castle
ISBN 978 0 7496 6698 9

TALES OF ROBIN HOOD

Robin and the Knight
ISBN 978 0 7496 6699 6

Robin and the Monk
ISBN 978 0 7496 6700 9

Robin and the Silver Arrow
ISBN 978 0 7496 6703 0

Robin and the Friar
ISBN 978 0 7496 6702 3

FAIRY TALES

The Emperor's New Clothes
ISBN 978 0 7496 7421 2

Cinderella
ISBN 978 0 7496 7417 5

Snow White
ISBN 978 0 7496 7418 2

Jack and the Beanstalk
ISBN 978 0 7496 7422 9

The Three Billy Goats Gruff
ISBN 978 0 7496 7420 5

The Pied Piper of Hamelin
ISBN 978 0 7496 7419 9

Goldilocks and the Three Bears
ISBN 978 0 7496 7903 3

Hansel and Gretel
ISBN 978 0 7496 7904 0

The Three Little Pigs
ISBN 978 0 7496 7905 7

Rapunzel
ISBN 978 0 7496 7906 4

Little Red Riding Hood
ISBN 978 0 7496 7907 1

Rumpelstiltskin
ISBN 978 0 7496 7908 8

HISTORIES

Toby and the Great Fire of London
ISBN 978 0 7496 7410 6

Pocahontas the Peacemaker
ISBN 978 0 7496 7411 3

Grandma's Seaside Bloomers
ISBN 978 0 7496 7412 0

Hoorah for Mary Seacole
ISBN 978 0 7496 7413 7

Remember the 5th of November
ISBN 978 0 7496 7414 4

Tutankhamun and the Golden Chariot
ISBN 978 0 7496 7415 1

MYTHS

Icarus, the Boy Who Flew
ISBN 978 0 7496 7992 7 *
ISBN 978 0 7496 8000 8

Perseus and the Snake Monster
ISBN 978 0 7496 7993 4 *
ISBN 978 0 7496 8001 5

Odysseus and the Wooden Horse
ISBN 978 0 7496 7994 1 *
ISBN 978 0 7496 8002 2

Persephone and the Pomegranate Seeds
ISBN 978 0 7496 7995 8 *
ISBN 978 0 7496 8003 9

Romulus and Remus
ISBN 978 0 7496 7996 5 *
ISBN 978 0 7496 8004 6

Thor's Hammer
ISBN 978 0 7496 7997 2*
ISBN 978 0 7496 8005 3

No Dinner for Anansi
ISBN 978 0 7496 7998 9 *
ISBN 978 0 7496 8006 0

Gelert the Brave
ISBN 978 0 7496 7999 6*
ISBN 978 0 7496 8007 7

STORIES OF RELIGION

The Good Samaritan
ISBN 978 0 7496 8369 6*
ISBN 978 0 7496 8375 7

The Loaves and the Fishes
ISBN 978 0 7496 8370 2*
ISBN 978 0 7496 8376 4

The Prince and Holika the Witch
ISBN 978 0 7496 8371 9*
ISBN 978 0 7496 8377 1

The Birth of Krishna
ISBN 978 0 7496 8368 9 *
ISBN 978 0 7496 8374 0

The Flight from Makkah
ISBN 978 0 7496 8373 3*
ISBN 978 0 7496 8379 5

The Great Night Journey
ISBN 978 0 7496 8372 6*
ISBN 978 0 7496 8378 8

For more details go to:
www.franklinwatts.co.uk

* **hardback**